Chester A. Arthur

Chester A. Arthur

Dan Elish

AMERICA'S
21ST
PRESIDENT

Children's Press®
A Division of Scholastic Inc.
New York / Toronto / London / Auckland / Sydney
Mexico City / New Delhi / Hong Kong
Danbury, Connecticut

Library of Congress Cataloging-in-Publication Data

Elish, Dan.
    Chester A. Arthur / by Dan Elish.
       p. cm.—(Encyclopedia of presidents. Second series)
Includes bibliographical references and index.
  ISBN 0-516-22961-3
    1. Arthur, Chester Alan, 1829–1886—Juvenile literature. 2. Presidents—
United States—Biography—Juvenile literature. I. Title. II. Series.
E692.E45 2004
973.8'4'092—dc22   2004003278

Contents

Gentleman Boss ————————————

Chester A. Arthur, the 21st president of the United States, was the ultimate big city New York politician. A likable man with a good head for management, Arthur served as quartermaster general of the state of New York during the Civil War and rose quickly in the ranks of the New York State Republican party. He was appointed to one of the most powerful positions in the federal government as the head of the New York customhouse. Because of his good manners and his ability to get things done behind the scenes, he was called the "Gentleman Boss."

Despite his successful career, Arthur never aspired to be president. In 1880, he was nominated to run for vice president with presidential candidate James Garfield. The two men favored different factions of their party and disagreed on major issues, but together they made a *balanced ticket* to appeal to Republican voters in different factions and regions. They were elected, but when President Garfield died only six months into his term, many Americans were shocked.

"Chet Arthur? President of the United States?" one horrified citizen cried. "Good God!" Arthur's reputation had been tarnished before he became vice president by accusations of corruption in the New York customhouse. Many worried that he was not honest enough for the job. Arthur surprised his detractors. From the day he set foot in the White House, he seemed determined to do what was right for the country. He supported prosecution of corrupt government officials, and he signed the Pendleton Civil Service Reform Act. The act reduced the power of political parties to appoint faithful party workers to government positions whether or not they were qualified.

By the end of Arthur's term, many in the country applauded his performance. Prominent author Mark Twain wrote, "I am but one in 55,000,000; still, in the opinion of this one-fifty-five-millionth of the country's population, it would be hard indeed to better President Arthur's administration."

Danced for Joy

Chester Arthur's father, William, was born in northern Ireland in 1796. In 1818, he moved to Canada. There he found a job teaching school in a settlement

A reconstruction of the small cottage in Fairfield, Vermont, where Chester Arthur was born in 1829.

15 miles (24 kilometers) from the United States border. He soon met a young woman from Vermont named Malvina Stone, and they were married in 1821. William Arthur became a minister in the Baptist Church in 1828 and moved his growing family to Fairfield, Vermont. On October 5, 1829, their first son was born. He was welcomed by four older sisters. William was thrilled to finally have a son. "And think of it!" a shocked neighbor said, "When I announced the boy to Elder Arthur, he danced up and down the room." The parents named their new son Chester Alan.

William Arthur was a man of passionate beliefs. He believed deeply that slavery was a moral evil, and was an *abolitionist*, a believer that slavery should be outlawed in the United States. In the pulpit, he took every opportunity to express his strong views on slavery and other issues. In addition, he was not gentle with his congregation. If someone dozed during one of his sermons, William wasn't shy—he would awaken the person with a loud, sarcastic remark. Perhaps because of his strong views and his prickly personality, William Arthur never stayed long in one place. When Chester was a child, the family moved five times in nine years. In 1839, when Chester was ten, the family settled in Union Village (now Greenwich), New York, a small village north of the city of Albany and about 12 miles (19 km) from the New York–Vermont border.

Slavery

In 1776, America's founding fathers met in Philadelphia to discuss whether they wanted to break away from British rule and create a new nation. Thomas Jefferson wrote in the Declaration of Independence that American citizens should be entitled to "life, liberty, and the pursuit of happiness." Unfortunately, these noble ideas pertained only to white people. The Founding Fathers—who did so much to advance the cause of freedom—owned about 1,400 African American slaves among them. As time went on, plantation owners in the southern states depended heavily on the labor of slaves. At the same time, more and more northerners came to think that slavery was wrong. Disagreement over the institution of slavery was a major cause of the Civil War, which began in 1861.

☆ ★ ☆

School Years

In Union Village, "Chet" Arthur went to school at a local academy. In 1844, when he was 14, the family moved again, to the small city of Schenectady. There he attended a school called the Lyceum, where he got into his first political dispute, an argument over his political hero, Senator Henry Clay of Kentucky. Clay was a leader of the Whig party. One day after school, a group of his classmates began criticizing Henry Clay. Chester stepped in to defend his hero. Arthur later wrote, "I have been in many a political battle since then, but none livelier, or that more thoroughly enlisted [involved] me."

In the fall of 1845, Chester entered Union College in Schenectady. Even though he was not quite 16, he enrolled as a second-year student. Students were expected to keep to a strict schedule, but Chester did find time to get into his share of mischief. Records show that he was caught jumping on and off slow-moving trains in a nearby train yard. Once he was punished for throwing the school bell into the Erie Canal. Yet he also participated in the school's debating society and wrote short stories and editorials for the school newspaper. In one essay, Chester showed that he was his father's son by condemning "the disastrous effects of slavery." In 1848, he was elected to Phi Beta Kappa, a prestigious honor

Teacher Arthur

Years later, one of Arthur's former students, Asa Stillman, recalled that as a boy he hated to recite poems in front of the class. One day Arthur ordered him to stay after school. Asa expected to be punished. Instead, Arthur wrote out a simple verse and helped Asa learn it by heart. The next day, the boy recited the poem perfectly in class, much to his delight.

Asa grew up to be a successful doctor. After Arthur became president, Asa showed the handwritten verse to a reporter. He said that he so admired his former teacher that he had named his son Chester Arthur Stillman.

☆ ☆ ☆

The Nott Memorial Building at Union College, from which Arthur graduated in 1848. A statue of Arthur is visible at the lower left.

society, and graduated from Union College. At the ceremony he delivered a speech called "The Destiny of Genius."

After college, Chester moved back home. He got a job teaching school and began studying law on his own. By 1853, he had saved enough money from his $35-a-month salary to move to New York City.

Lawyer in New York

In New York, Arthur went to work for Culver & Parker, a small law firm. Erastus D. Culver, one of the partners, was an old family friend of the Arthurs. Like Arthur's father, Culver was an ardent abolitionist. In fact, it was even rumored that Culver had assisted with the Underground Railroad, the secret organization that helped slaves escape from their owners and flee to Canada.

Under Culver's guidance, Arthur finished his law studies. In 1854, the law firm filed papers confirming that Arthur was of "good moral character" and had studied the law for more than a year in its offices. On May 1, Arthur was licensed to practice law in New York State. Erastus Culver invited him to join the firm of Culver & Parker.

During his years with the firm, Arthur participated in two influential cases, both of which involved African Americans. The first had begun even before

A view of Broadway in New York City about the time Chester Arthur arrived in the city to study law.

he arrived in the city. In 1852, southerners Jonathan and Juliet Lemmon arrived in New York by ship with eight slaves whom they were transporting from Virginia to Texas. While waiting for the next ship to Texas, the slaves were discovered in a rooming house on Carlisle Street. Since New York did not allow slavery or the importation of slaves, the slaves appeared before Judge Elijah Paine and asked to be *emancipated*, or freed. The Lemmons argued in court that they still owned the slaves, who were simply in transit between Virginia and Texas, two states that allowed slavery. Judge Paine was not convinced. On November 15, he ruled that the slaves should be freed.

The people of the South were outraged. It seemed to them that New York was bending the law to free slaves. The Virginia legislature was so angry that it authorized its *attorney general* (the state's highest legal officer) to appeal the New York judge's decision. In 1855 the New York attorney general appointed Erastus Culver to help argue for freeing the slaves. Arthur served as Culver's assistant and helped prepare the case. In December 1857, the court upheld Judge Paine's decision. In 1860, New York's highest court agreed. The slaves were officially free.

The second case concerned an incident that happened in 1854, soon after Arthur received his law license. One Sunday morning, Elizabeth Jennings, an African American schoolteacher, was riding a streetcar on the way to church. A conductor asked her to get off the car, since black riders were not allowed. Jennings refused, and when the conductor tried to push her off the car, she resisted. Finally the conductor gained the help of a policeman, who forced Jennings to get off.

The Jennings family decided to sue the streetcar company, and they engaged the firm now called Culver, Parker & Arthur as their lawyers. Arthur argued the case and succeeded in winning a judgment of $250 and court costs against the streetcar company (about $5,000 in today's money). The case received wide publicity, and in the following months, the major streetcar companies in the city ended their ban on African American passengers. It was a remarkable victory. No doubt William Arthur, the fervent abolitionist, was proud of his son.

Courtship and Business ─────────────

Like many single men in New York, Arthur lived in a boardinghouse with other young men. They ate their meals there and spent time together, discussing their careers, politics, and other subjects of interest. In 1856, Arthur struck up a friendship with a medical student named Dabney Herndon. One day he went with Herndon to visit Herndon's relatives. There he met Herndon's cousin, a charming and talented young woman named Nell Herndon. She was 19 years old and was living in New York with her family. That summer, they spent time together in Saratoga, New York, a popular vacation community. Within a year, Chester Arthur proposed marriage to Nell, and she accepted.

Arthur was also setting out on a new course as a lawyer. In 1856, he left Culver, Parker & Arthur to set up a new firm with his

Ellen Herndon, known to her friends as Nell, was born in Virginia to a distinguished family. Her father had long served in the U.S. Navy and had led a pioneering expedition up the Amazon River. When Nell was young, her family lived in Washington, D.C., where her father helped establish the U.S. Naval Observatory.

Nell's great interest was music, and she was becoming a much admired singer, both in choral groups and in solo performances. In 1856, her father had left the navy and became captain of a mail packet that sailed long distances out of New York. The family moved to the city. Nell's mother, Frances Herndon, was soon a member of New York's high society.

Arthur met Ellen Herndon, the daughter of a famous naval captain, in New York in the mid-1850s. They were married in 1859.

Chet Arthur came from a humbler background, but he had already gained many social graces. He dressed stylishly and seemed a dashing figure. After their marriage, Nell proved an asset to Arthur's career. She was comfortable in the company of rich and influential people and served as a gracious hostess at dinner parties. During their years in New York, the Arthurs were among the most charming couples at any gathering.

☆ ☆ ☆

good friend Henry D. Gardiner. In 1857, soon after Arthur was engaged to Nell Herndon, he and Gardiner decided to make a business trip to the western frontier in Kansas. Attracted by stories of riches made in real estate, they hoped to invest in Kansas land, buying undeveloped land cheaply and selling it later for more money to settlers arriving from the East.

Arthur and Gardiner chose a terrible time to visit Kansas. Three years earlier, in 1854, President Franklin Pierce signed the Kansas-Nebraska Act, which allowed the citizens of those two new states to decide by a simple vote whether they would allow slavery or not. Nebraska quickly voted to be a free state, but the people of Kansas were evenly divided. Proslavery leaders were eager for the state to vote for slavery. Antislavery leaders were just as eager for the state to vote against slavery. Both sides sent hundreds of new settlers to the state, hoping to influence the vote. Soon fighting broke out between the two sides. Proslavery and antislavery forces set up competing governments. During the unrest, which became known as "Bleeding Kansas," more than 200 people died.

Arthur and Gardiner soon decided that Bleeding Kansas was not a good place to invest in land. Arthur was at a political meeting that ended in gunfire. Later, he was stopped and threatened by proslavery *vigilantes*, a group of armed men who took the law into their own hands. Until law and order was established, the land would be worthless. Then Arthur received a telegram from Nell in New

On his visit to Kansas, Arthur learned that proslavery and antislavery forces were conducting a small-scale war for control of the territory. Even this "peace conference" quickly led to violence.

York. She reported that her father had been lost at sea when his ship sank off the coast of North Carolina. Arthur and Gardiner hurried home.

Thurlow Weed's "Machine" ─────────────

About the time Arthur first arrived in New York City, a new political party was being born. The two traditional parties, Democrats and Whigs, tried to say as little as possible about slavery, since they had members in both the North and the South. In 1854, dissatisfied northerners who strongly opposed the spread of slavery began forming the Republican party. Arthur attended one of the first Republican meetings in New York in 1854, and in 1855 he served as a poll inspector on election day. In 1856, Republicans nominated John C. Frémont, a famous explorer, to run for president, and Arthur campaigned for him energetically. Frémont lost the election, but Arthur continued to work for the Republican party in New York City.

New York City was changing rapidly. Waves of immigrants had arrived from Ireland and Germany, and thousands had settled in the city. The new immigrants often lived in poverty, but they soon became a political force. Leaders of the city's Democratic party realized that the immigrants could help elect Democratic candidates to office. Local leaders helped immigrants organize and solve pressing problems of housing and sanitation. By 1860, many Irish and German families were loyal Democrats. They knew that if they campaigned for the party and contributed to it, they would be rewarded with city jobs and eventually with election to local offices.

The Republican party was not strong in New York City, but it had a powerful base in the rest of New York State. Soon after its founding, Thurlow Weed, an experienced political operative, took control of the party. Working from the state

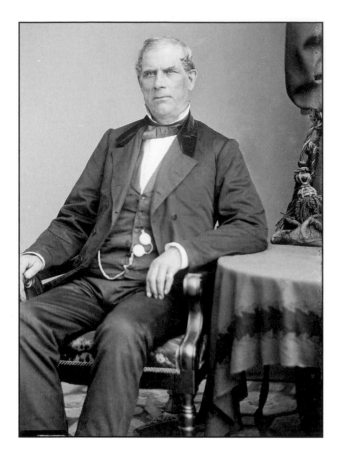

Thurlow Weed was the most powerful Republican boss in New York State when Arthur entered politics.

capital in Albany, Weed gained so much power that he was called "the dictator." Like Democratic organizers in New York City, Weed also used the *spoils system*—giving out government jobs and contracts only to party members to reward their services and loyalty. Those who received jobs were required to pay a percentage of their salaries back to the party's campaign fund. Some of this money found its way into the pockets of the party leaders.

In areas where Democrats and Republicans were evenly represented, the party organizations used every available means to win elections. The party in power often had the chance to "stuff" ballot boxes with extra votes for its candidate or to "lose" ballots cast by opponents. On election day, the organizations sent "heelers" to opposition neighborhoods to scare voters away from the polling places with threats of violence.

Arthur was soon caught up in these free-for-all political battles. As a committed party worker, he gained the attention of Thurlow Weed himself. In 1860, Weed recommended Arthur to Republican governor Edwin Morgan. Morgan appointed him engineer in chief in the state militia. It was a *ceremonial position*—it had few powers, but required Arthur to attend occasional public events wearing a uniform. Arthur took on his new title in January 1861.

By that time, the nation was on the brink of civil war. In November 1860, Republican Abraham Lincoln was elected president on a platform that pledged to stop the spread of slavery. In December, the first southern states *seceded* from the United States. Their representatives in Washington resigned their posts, and state authorities began

Fast Facts

THE CIVIL WAR

Who: The United States (the Union, or the North) against the Confederate States of America (the South), made up of southern states that had seceded from the Union

When: April 12, 1861–May 1865

Why: Southern states, believing the election of Abraham Lincoln threatened states' rights and slavery, seceded from the United States and fought for their independence. The North fought to restore the southern states to the Union, and later to end slavery.

Where: Confederate and border states, and in coastal waters

Outcome: The Confederate Army of Northern Virginia surrendered to Union forces April 9, 1865, ending the major fighting. The victorious North passed legislation that abolished slavery, gave civil rights to former slaves, and put defeated states under military rule. Efforts to reconstruct the South continued until 1877.

seizing U.S. military bases and supplies within their borders. By March 1861, when Lincoln took office, the southern states had formed their own Confederate States of America. In April, Confederate troops fired on Fort Sumter, a U.S. base in Charleston, South Carolina, and the Civil War began.

Arthur the Administrator ————————————

The Union, now made up only of northern states, was confident that it would easily win the war. The North had greater manpower, greater industrial strength, more money, and thousands of miles of railroad tracks to move troops and supplies. The Confederacy soon surprised the North. In July 1861, Union forces suffered a shocking defeat at Bull Run in northern Virginia. When Confederate troops counterattacked the Union forces, inexperienced northern soldiers ran for their lives. One newsman wrote, "All sense of manhood seemed to be forgotten. . . . Every impediment to flight was cast aside. Rifles, bayonets, pistols . . . cartridge-boxes, canteens, blankets, and overcoats lined the road."

Even before the defeat at Bull Run, President Lincoln asked the northern governors to raise 75,000 volunteers to fight. New York State appropriated $3 million to arm 30,000 troops. Arthur was appointed to a position in the state quartermaster general's office, whose job was to feed, clothe, shelter, and equip the thousands of new recruits. It was a staggering task. Arthur had no experience

Arthur In uniform during the Civil War, when he served as state quartermaster general.

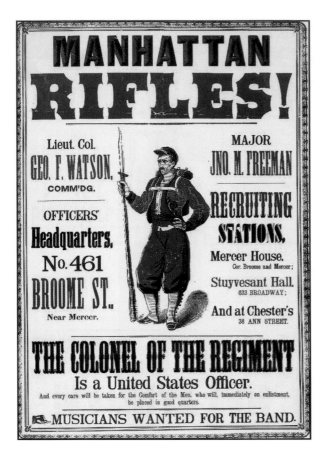

Dozens of organizations were recruiting volunteers to fight in the Civil War. Arthur's job was to provide food, clothing, and shelter while they trained.

managing large groups of people or supplies, but he proved to be a hard worker and an excellent administrator.

Regiments of the militia were recruited by individuals, who advertised widely, seeking volunteers. A full regiment had about 800 men. Individual regiments might include many volunteers from the same profession (such as firemen) or from the same neighborhood or national background. Some were carefully drilled and disciplined by their officers, but others were not.

One of Arthur's jobs was to deal with the regiments that didn't follow orders. One regiment was organized by Billy Wilson, a Democratic alderman from one of New York's toughest neighborhoods. Wilson's regiment refused to eat army rations. Instead, it went on a rampage, stealing food from inns and stores. When Arthur ordered Wilson to disband his regiment, Wilson replied, "Neither you nor the governor has nothing to do with me. I'm a colonel in the U.S. army, and you've got no right to order me." Arthur wasn't intimidated. He eventually threw Wilson into a chair and had him arrested.

Another regiment that caused trouble was the Ellsworth's Fire Zouaves, made up mostly of New York City firemen. They dressed in colorful uniforms and could drill smartly on parade, but they were also famous for their lack of discipline. When they were sent to help defend Washington, D.C., one newspaper reported that they "broke into taverns" and "terrified old ladies." Arthur ordered

The Ellsworth's Zouaves, made up of New York City firefighters, march off to war in 1861. They caused so much trouble in Washington that Arthur had them reassigned to duties elsewhere.

the regiment back to New York in September. He later disbanded it and placed the troops in other regiments.

Quartermaster General

By the summer of 1862, the future of the Union cause looked bleak. The Confederacy continued to defeat Union armies in battle after battle, and President Lincoln was forced to call for 300,000 more troops. New York State was asked to raise 120,000 new volunteers to be sent to the front immediately. Soon after Lincoln's call went out, Arthur was promoted to quartermaster general, taking full charge of supplying and housing the thousands of new recruits.

Family Tensions

Like many families during the Civil War, the Arthur family had divided loyalties. Most of Nell's family favored the Confederacy, and some fought in the Confederate army. They were horrified that her husband was "an officer in Lincoln's army." Arthur joked about his "little rebel wife," but when he traveled to the South to inspect conditions of the troops, he checked up on Nell's family. In July 1862, he arranged for his old friend (and Nell's cousin), Dabney Herndon, to be released from a Union prison.

☆ ☆ ☆

Once again, Arthur rose to the occasion. Temporary housing was the first big problem. During the winter, standard army tents didn't protect the shivering recruits from the cold. Arthur arranged for soldiers to be housed in private quarters, then arranged for the construction of 200 emergency barracks. He requisitioned wood from local providers, then shipped the wood back when the barracks were no longer needed. After housing, clothing, and feeding the new troops, he negotiated special contracts with railroads to transport them to the battlefronts as quickly as possible.

Arthur served as quartermaster general until 1863, when Governor Morgan was voted out of office. The governor recalled that Arthur "displayed not only great executive ability and unbending integrity, but great knowledge of army regulations. He can say no . . . without giving offense." Nearly 50 years later, Arthur's son Alan told an interviewer, "I think my father's greatest work was as quartermaster general of New York State."

Chapter 3

Machine Politician

The war years were a tumultuous time for the Arthur family. Their first son, William, was born in 1860, but in July 1863, before his third birthday, he died suddenly. "Nell is brokenhearted," Arthur wrote his brother. "I fear much for her health. You know how her heart was wrapped up in her dear boy."

Only days after William's death, New York City was rocked by the most violent riot in its history. To raise 300,000 more troops for the Union cause, President Lincoln had called for a draft, which would force men in the North to serve in the army. The first drawing of names for the draft occurred on July 11. Many of the names picked in New York were those of Irish immigrants. The next day, angry crowds swarmed into the streets to protest the draft. For three days, they attacked and looted stores and threatened those they considered enemies. African Americans were special targets of their anger. President Lincoln was forced to send Union troops to restore order. By the time the riots ended, several dozen people were killed, and $1.5 million of damage was done.

Arthur was no longer quartermaster general, so the responsibility of providing for new recruits belonged to someone else. He was soon busy getting his law practice back on track. His years in government service had taken a toll on his finances, and he was eager to increase his income. His firm was soon representing businesses and individuals who had war claims against the government.

His first love remained politics. He spent many evenings working for the Republican machine. One of his main hangouts was the home of Tom Murphy, one of the city's Republican leaders. One frequent visitor to Murphy's later recalled, "Sooner or later, but always unfailing, was the well-known ring and footstep of General Arthur, as we used to call him. Always smiling and affectionate in his manner toward his friends." Arthur was always ready with a funny story, and he enjoyed staying up late talking politics. As time went on, he spent more and more evenings out, rose late in the mornings, and spent fewer hours practicing law. He was beginning to see ways to succeed and prosper in politics.

In 1863, times were not promising for Republicans in New York. The state and the city were governed by Democrats. Even so, Republicans were not defeated. Arthur's mentor, former governor Edwin Morgan, was elected to the

U.S. Senate in 1863, and another ambitious Republican, Roscoe Conkling, was beginning his rise to power in the state. Arthur's association with these leaders and with prominent businessmen in New York City helped him rise rapidly both in politics and in society. In 1867, he was elected to membership in the exclusive Century Club, a meeting place for some of New York's richest and most influential people.

Roscoe Conkling

Roscoe Conkling was one of the most flamboyant men of his era. He stood 6 feet 3 inches (1.9 meters) tall and had a wavy red beard. He wore polka-dot ties, kerchiefs in his upper jacket pocket, and high white hats. One observer said, "He walked along with the air of a prince." He was also a brilliant public speaker.

After serving as mayor of Utica, New York, Conkling was elected to Congress in 1858 and 1860, but lost his seat in the Democratic landslide of 1862. The same age as Chester Arthur, Conkling devoted his years out of office to organizing and taking control of the state Republican party. He would soon be known as the "boss" of New York Republicans. His career would intertwine with Arthur's in unexpected ways.

In 1867, Conkling was elected to the U.S. Senate from New York. The next year, he was a leading campaigner to nominate General Ulysses S. Grant for

Roscoe Conkling (above) was the most powerful Republican in New York when he befriended former general Ulysses S. Grant (right) and helped him get elected president. Grant appointed Conkling's lieutenant, Chester Arthur, to direct the New York customhouse.

president. Grant won the nomination and was elected. When Grant took office as president the following spring, Conkling and his friends were allowed to control appointments to thousands of federal jobs in New York State.

Arthur became one of Conkling's most trusted lieutenants, working behind the scenes in New York City. As in the days of Thurlow Weed, the party helped those who supported it with their contributions, their time, and their votes. In 1868 Arthur was appointed chairman of the state Republican executive committee. The following year, he was appointed to the New York City Tax Commission. The job offered steady pay, but greatly reduced his income. The Arthurs now had a second son, Alan (born in 1864), and hoped that Chester's loyal service to the party would result in an even better government appointment.

To the Victors Belong the Spoils

In the mid-1860s, the federal government employed 53,000 workers, who were paid a total of $30 million a year. A newly elected president had the power to replace thousands of these workers with appointees of his own choosing. He often appointed close friends and supporters to the highest positions, but allowed the state party leaders to choose appointees to positions in their state. State officials used these appointments to reward their supporters and strengthen their party.

☆☆☆

When President Grant took office in 1869, New York Republicans argued fiercely over who should be appointed to run the New York customhouse. Senator Conkling recommended Arthur's old friend Thomas Murphy, and Grant appointed him. Two years later, however, New York City's Democratic leader, William "Boss" Tweed, was convicted of cheating the city out of millions of dollars. The public was appalled. During Tweed's trial, it was revealed that Murphy had made various real estate deals with Tweed, and Murphy was forced to resign from his customhouse position. Conkling recommended Chester Arthur, and Grant agreed. The appointment as Collector of the Port of New York was a reward to Arthur for his services to the party and a recognition of his ability as a manager.

Not all Republicans were overjoyed with his appointment. A group of reform-minded Republicans in New York objected to Conkling's machine politics. Horace Greeley, publisher of

Horace Greeley, a reform-minded Republican, opposed Arthur's appointment as head of the New York customhouse. In 1872 he ran for president against President Grant and was defeated.

the *New York Tribune*, believed that candidates for government jobs should be chosen by *merit* (appropriate education and experience), not by political affiliation. In an editorial, Greeley wrote that Arthur was not "personally objectionable," but argued that Arthur had risen to power in a corrupt system and should not receive the job. Greeley's comment did not surprise or trouble Arthur at the time. He fully agreed with Conkling's methods of operation.

Arthur Runs the Customhouse

November of 1871 was a fine month for the Arthurs. On the 21st, Nell gave birth to a daughter, Ellen Herndon Arthur. A few days later, Arthur started work at his new job. The New York customhouse was a huge operation. It monitored the arrival of goods in the Port of New York, including all ports in New York State and northern New Jersey. Its main responsibility was to collect *tariffs*, taxes on imported goods. In the early 1870s, the tariffs came to more than $100 million a year and represented an important part of the federal government's income. The customhouse was the largest federal office in the nation, and employed more than a thousand workers.

For the Republicans, control of the customhouse meant the chance to offer hundreds of jobs to faithful Republicans from the New York City region. The jobs would help confirm the appointees' loyalty to the party. In addition, they would be expected to return a small percentage of their salaries to the party, filling the treasury with money for future campaigns and perhaps paying party officials as well.

For Arthur personally, the job as Collector of the Port of New York brought a huge income. During his first three years, he received a salary of $12,000 a year (about $250,000 in present-day value). In addition, he received a percentage of the fines and penalties that customs inspectors collected. He earned more than $50,000 (about $1 million today) each of those years. The "percentage" system was discontinued in 1874, but Arthur's salary still allowed him to support a luxurious lifestyle. He moved his family into a fine brownstone on New York's Lexington Avenue and employed five servants. Arthur also liked to dress well and spent freely on clothes. His bill for hats between February 13 and October 28, 1875, was $125 (about $2,500 today).

Arthur became a familiar figure in New York society. He dressed handsomely, had elegant manners, and prized good food and wines. His wife Nell was beautiful and cultured. He also seemed comfortable with his responsibilities at the customhouse, impressing even the most prosperous business leaders. One observer wrote, "He possessed a judicial mind, well balanced in every respect, which caused his decisions to be almost invariably right."

In some ways, Arthur's responsibilities were larger than his rich friends knew. In addition to managing the customhouse, he helped run the New York

This building served as the headquarters of the New York customhouse when Arthur became its head in 1871.

Republican party. Often he left a late-night social event to spend a few hours with political associates in the Conkling machine. Working most of the night, he sometimes did not arrive at his office until afternoon. Because he was away from home so much, he and Nell, who did not share his passion for politics, grew further and further apart.

Scandals in Washington

As the former general in chief of Union forces in the Civil War, Ulysses S. Grant entered the presidency as the most popular man in the nation (although some in the South still hated him). Through his first term, his popularity remained high, and he easily won re-election in 1872. By this time, however, there were signs that all was not well.

Although Grant had been a brilliant general, he was a political beginner. He had never held an elective office before and had not worked in politics. It gradually became clear that he was a trusting man who followed the advice of his friends and political allies. Unfortunately, some of these friends were making themselves rich at the government's expense. Two high-flying businessmen, James Fisk and Jay Gould, used a casual friendship with Grant to influence government policy on selling gold. Although Grant discovered the plot and foiled it at the last moment, the price of gold suddenly dropped, ruining many innocent investors.

Later, it was revealed that members of the Grant administration were making millions of dollars by neglecting to charge federal taxes on whiskey. The whiskey-makers rewarded the government workers handsomely for saving them money. Grant's first vice president, Schuyler Colfax, was caught in a plot to skim huge profits from the construction of the country's first transcontinental railroad.

Reformers also complained about the spoils system, which placed politically connected but incompetent workers in government jobs.

A Reformer in the White House ————————

On December 17, 1875, Arthur was appointed to a second term as head of the customhouse. Meanwhile, things were not going well for New York's Republican party. In 1874, the nation's economy went into a downturn. That fall, voters angered by bad economic times and the scandals in the Grant administration began to elect Democrats. Democrat Samuel Tilden, who had exposed the corruption of the infamous Tweed Ring in his own party, was elected governor of New York. With the state in Democratic hands, the Conkling machine depended even more on the jobs provided by the customhouse. Even though bad times reduced business, Arthur was under enormous pressure to create more jobs for deserving Republicans.

As the presidential election of 1876 approached, Boss Conkling began to worry that a Democrat might be elected president. He announced his support for running President Grant for a third term. Even though Grant remained popular, the scandals in his administration had reduced his political support. In the end, the Republicans nominated a reform candidate, Ohio governor Rutherford B.

Republican president Rutherford B. Hayes won the disputed election of 1876.

Hayes, to run for president. That fall he defeated New York governor Samuel Tilden in one of the closest presidential elections in history.

President Hayes soon proved that he was serious about reform. He declared that the spoils system "ought to be abolished" and publicly urged civil service reform. He planned to investigate appointment practices in federal offices, and his first target was the New York customhouse. Hayes appointed a commission to investigate Chester Arthur's preserve. The commission heard hundreds of witnesses, including Arthur, who was called to testify for six hours. Some witnesses claimed that the customhouse's address on Hanover Street should be changed to "Hand-Over-Street" because of the "voluntary contributions" workers were required to give to the Republican party. Others testified that the customhouse had too many workers on staff.

Arthur "stonewalled" the investigation, revealing as little as possible about his appointment practices. When the commission urged him to fire many employees who rarely did any useful work, Arthur studied the situation. He reported that "by putting the force upon a basis of the closest economy," he could reduce the workforce by 66—a very small reduction in a force of more than a thousand.

The commission report strongly criticized the customhouse. It said that too many jobs were given out based on political connections. It criticized the practice of requiring "voluntary contributions" and concluded that the entire operation was overstaffed with poorly qualified workers. The commission did not accuse Arthur of taking bribes himself or using threats to collect contributions, but it did state that the customhouse was poorly managed and riddled with underhand dealings.

In September 1877, Hayes asked Arthur to resign. Feeling that he had been unfairly criticized, Arthur refused. Meanwhile, Roscoe Conkling was working feverishly to rally support in Congress. He wanted to make it politically difficult for Hayes to fire Arthur. Hayes held his ground. Finally, in July 1878, after Congress had adjourned, the president suspended Arthur. Conkling was furious, but he was unable to gain enough support to get Arthur reinstated. Greatly embarrassed, Arthur had no choice but to step down.

A Sad Season

Arthur returned to the practice of law and continued his work in the state Republican party. In 1879 he helped engineer the re-election of Roscoe Conkling to the U.S. Senate and the election of Republican Alonzo Cornell as governor of New York. It appeared for the moment that Conkling had regained control of the New York Republicans.

Nell Arthur died in January 1880, only months before her husband was nominated for vice president.

In January 1880, Arthur made one of his frequent trips to Albany, the state capital. While he was gone, Nell Arthur performed one evening at a concert in New York. On the way home, she got chilled and became suddenly ill with pneumonia. Arthur hurried back to the city, but by the time he arrived, Nell had lost consciousness. She died a few hours later.

Even though the Arthurs had grown apart, Chester was devastated by his wife's death and felt deep remorse that his obsession with politics often kept him away from home. In addition to her husband, Nell left their two children, Alan, who was 15, and Ellen, who was 8. Although Arthur would soon be president, without Nell his success seemed somewhat hollow. As he told one friend, "Honors to me now are not what they once were."

Stalwarts and Moderates ───────

During the administration of Hayes, from 1877 to 1881, the lines between Republican factions hardened. Roscoe Conkling was the undisputed leader of the "Stalwarts," who had come to power during the years of Grant's presidency. They revered and supported Grant, and they continued to support strong measures against southern states that denied basic freedoms to African Americans. At the same time, they prided themselves in being practical "hard-nosed" politicians. They were against reforming civil service laws and insisted that the victorious party had a right to appoint its own government employees.

The moderate wing of the party favored more lenient treatment of the South and moderate civil service reforms. Stalwarts ridiculed the moderates, calling them "Half-Breeds," suggesting that they were trying to be Republicans and Democrats at the same time. The leader of the moderates was Maine senator James G. Blaine. He and Conkling had been mortal enemies for many years, refusing to speak to each other even when they served together in the Senate. In addition to disagreeing on policy matters, they were rivals for Republican patronage. Each of them wanted to decide which Republicans would receive high appointments in Republican administrations.

As the 1880 presidential election drew near, Republicans were faced with making a new choice. Rutherford Hayes had pledged to serve for only one term. Now the battle would be fought between Stalwarts and moderates. Roscoe Conkling announced the Stalwarts' support once again for the nomination of Ulysses S. Grant. After leaving office, Grant had traveled around the world, welcomed by huge crowds wherever he went. He received another large welcome when he returned to the United States in the fall of 1879. In Philadelphia he was greeted by 60,000 well-wishers, and the city sponsored a huge parade in his honor. Arthur, now president of the New York Republican Central Committee, rallied New York Stalwarts behind Grant.

The rival candidate was James G. Blaine. Blaine's long record as a leader in Congress and his support for reform seemed to give him a good chance to win the nomination. There were questions about his past, however. Investigators suggested that he had personally profited from a corrupt business deal in the Grant years. The Stalwarts played up Blaine's weaknesses.

In 1880, dark-horse candidate James A. Garfield was nominated for president. To help gain the support of New York Republicans, Garfield chose Chester Arthur to run for vice president.

When the Republican convention began voting for a nominee, the two leading candidates divided the votes, and neither was able to win the required two-thirds majority. Conditions were right for a dark horse, a little-known candidate with few political enemies. That person was James Garfield, a longtime congressman from Ohio. Early in the convention, Garfield had made an eloquent nominating speech for another candidate, drawing more attention to himself than to the nominee. His eloquence and his support for moderate reforms attracted the delegates. On the 34th ballot, the Wisconsin delegation threw 16 votes to Garfield. Blaine let his supporters know they were free to vote for Garfield, and others began changing their votes. He won the nomination on the 36th ballot. Roscoe Conkling was not pleased. A reporter saw him walking "up and down the long aisle with energetic steps . . . often muttering aloud."

The Vice President

Garfield knew that to win the election he needed a united party. In particular, he could not win without carrying the state of New York, which then had more residents and electoral votes than any other state. In an effort to gain Stalwart support, he offered the vice presidential nomination to New York banker Levi P. Morton. After consulting with Conkling, who was still furious, Morton turned down the nomination.

Then representatives of Garfield sounded out Arthur. Would he like to be vice president? Arthur had worked closely with Conkling for years, but he felt no need to consult the boss about this question. Arthur still nursed a deep anger over what he felt was unfair treatment during the investigation of the customhouse. What better way to recover his good name than to be named to the national ticket?

Years later, a reporter described the scene when Arthur informed Conkling of the offer. "Well, sir," Conkling said, "you should drop it as you would a red hot shoe from the forge." He then added, "This trickster [Garfield] will be defeated before the country."

Arthur was not asking permission, however. He had already made up his mind. "The vice president is a greater honor than I ever dreamed of attaining," he said. "In a calmer moment you will look at this differently. . . . I shall accept the nomination and carry with me the majority of the delegation."

Many, Republicans and Democrats alike, were shocked by Arthur's nomination. The *Louisville Courier-Journal* carried a picture of Arthur with the caption, "Nominated at Chicago for the vice-presidency. Suspended by President Hayes from the New York Collectorship, that the office might be honestly administered." Some citizens even asked if they could vote for Garfield without voting for Arthur! Others were not so concerned. They said that a vice president has very

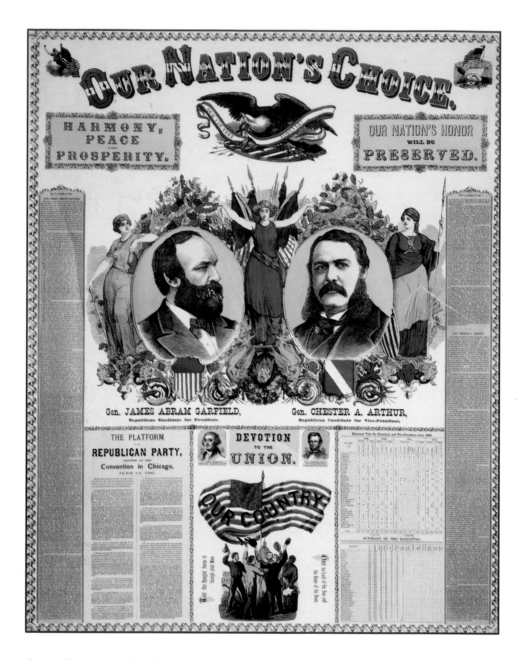

This Republican campaign broadsheet shows Garfield and Arthur and promises "harmony, peace, and prosperity."

limited responsibilities. The editor of *The Nation* magazine wrote, "There is no place in which his [Arthur's] powers of mischief will be so small as in the Vice Presidency. . . . It is true General Garfield, if elected, may die during his term of office, but this is too unlikely a contingency to be worth making extraordinary provision for."

Arthur silenced some of his critics by writing a public letter pledging his support for some sort of civil service reform. "Original appointments should be based on . . . fitness," he stated. "Positions of responsibility should . . . be filled by the promotion of worthy and efficient officers." He also enhanced his reputation by campaigning vigorously on Garfield's behalf. To win the election, the Republicans had to hold the states they had won four years earlier and win either

The Treaty of Fifth Avenue

During the campaign, James Garfield made a special trip to New York to meet with leaders of the Stalwart faction. The Stalwarts later claimed that Garfield agreed to give Stalwarts important positions in the new administration. This so-called Treaty of Fifth Avenue helped energize the Stalwarts to work for Garfield in New York. With their help, he carried the state by a paper-thin margin. Later, when Garfield did not appoint Stalwarts to the offices they expected, their anger helped begin a major political battle.

★★★

New York or Indiana, two states that had gone to the Democrat Tilden. Calling on his skills as a party professional, Arthur supervised fund-raising, coordinated rallies, and arranged for important members of the party to give speeches. He organized a campaign tour by Conkling and Grant through the Midwest. He also raised money by the tried-and-true method of requiring "voluntary contributions" from Republican officeholders.

In the end, Garfield and Arthur won an extremely close election. With 10 million votes cast, the Republicans won by only 7,018!

A cartoon shows the Republican candidates. Garfield (left), on a pedestal marked "troublesome record," has a small sign promoting himself. A tiny Chester Arthur stands on a pedestal marked "peculiar record" and holds a much larger sign supporting himself for vice president.

Waiting to Take Office ───────

The day after the election found Arthur at the Fifth Avenue Hotel in New York, receiving well-wishers and accepting congratulations. He was in a fine mood. Two years earlier he had been fired from one of the most important jobs in the federal government and disgraced before his friends and family. Now he was vice president, in a position to help the new Republican administration—and the Stalwarts.

James Garfield had different ideas, however. Ignoring his reported promises to the Stalwarts, the new president soon declared, "I will not tolerate nor act upon any understanding that anything has been pledged to a party, state, or person." He refused to appoint Stalwart leader and prominent New York banker Levi Morton as secretary of the treasury. Worse, he appointed Conkling's lifelong rival, James Blaine, as secretary of state. Roscoe Conkling was outraged. Arthur tried to appeal to Garfield on the behalf of various Stalwarts, but the president-elect listened to James Blaine.

President Garfield appointed moderate James G. Blaine, an enemy of the Stalwarts, to be secretary of state, the most powerful post in the president's cabinet.

During that winter Arthur's own reputation suffered a blow. At a political dinner in Delmonico's, a famous New York restaurant, Arthur made a rambling speech. He suggested that he had helped eke out a Republican victory in Indiana by buying votes. Then he said, "If it were not for the reporters [in the room], I would tell you the truth." The party goers, including ex-president Grant, howled with laughter. But when the speech was reported in the papers, it did Arthur little credit. *The Nation* wrote: "The cynicism of this, coming from such a veteran Machinist [machine politician] as Mr. Arthur, was not surprising."

Garfield's Presidency

Once Garfield was sworn in as president, the infighting between the Stalwarts and the moderates intensified. The showdown came over who would be appointed Collector of the Port of New York—Arthur's old job. Early in his term, Garfield appointed William H. Robertson, a New Yorker who was a well-known moderate and a supporter of Blaine.

Because the appointment required the approval of the Senate, Roscoe Conkling began a campaign against Robertson. Garfield refused to back down. He wrote to a friend, "This will settle the question of whether the President is registering clerk of the Senate or the Executive of the United States." Arthur tried to discuss the matter with the president, but he was powerless to affect the decision.

When Conkling refused to allow Robertson's nomination to come up for a vote, Garfield retaliated. He withdrew all other nominations awaiting approval, including many for Stalwarts. Seeing that he could not prevail in the Senate, Conkling made a dramatic move—he announced his resignation from the Senate, and moments later, his fellow senator from New York, Thomas Platt, also resigned. At the time, senators were elected by state legislatures, and Conkling was confident that the New York legislature would quickly re-elect him and Platt to their seats, administering a strong rebuke to Garfield. He learned to his sorrow that he had miscalculated.

With Conkling and Platt no longer in place, the Senate approved Robertson's appointment to the New York customhouse. Then the New York state legislature, hopelessly divided between Democrats, Stalwarts, and moderate Republicans, could not agree on whom to elect to the vacant seats. The battle continued through the early summer of 1881. Platt withdrew after a personal scandal ruined his reputation, but Conkling refused to quit. Arthur went to Albany to help lobby for his old boss. On July 2, Arthur and Conkling had just returned to New York City from Albany when they learned some shocking news. While walking through the Baltimore and Ohio train station in Washington, Garfield was shot by an assassin. He was gravely wounded.

In July 1881, President Garfield was shot in the waiting room of a Washington railway station by Charles Guiteau, a disappointed office-seeker.

A Summer of Waiting

When the assassin, Charles Guiteau, was caught moments after the shooting, he said, "Arthur is president, and I am a Stalwart." It turned out that Guiteau was a mentally unbalanced man who had visited the White House many times seeking appointment to high diplomatic positions. His applications were always turned down. In his own mind, he was a Stalwart, but he had no connection to Arthur or to any other Stalwart leader.

Arthur was visibly shaken by Garfield's shooting and overwhelmed by the prospect of becoming president, an office he never sought. As Garfield fought for his life, Arthur became further dismayed by a series of savage attacks against him in the nation's press. *The Nation* wrote, "It is out of this mess of filth [Stalwart dishonesty] that Mr. Arthur will go to the presidential chair in case of the President's death." Ex-president Hayes predicted, "Conkling will be the power behind the

After languishing for ten weeks, Garfield died on September 19, 1881, six and a half months after his inauguration.

Chester Arthur is sworn in as president in the parlor of his New York home after learning of Garfield's death.

throne." It was a view that many Americans shared. Still, Arthur made it clear that his only hopes were for Garfield's speedy recovery, saying at one point, "As the president gets better, I get better, too."

Doctors were unable to remove the bullet lodged in Garfield's back. He lingered all summer. Late in August, he asked to be moved to a summer cottage in Elberon, New Jersey, near the beach. For a few weeks, he seemed to rally, but on September 19, he took a turn for the worse. That night he died.

Arthur was at his home on Lexington Avenue in New York City. When reporters gathered at Arthur's door, his doorkeeper, Alec Powell, told them, "He is sitting alone in his room sobbing like a child, with his head on his desk and his face buried in his hands. I dare not disturb him."

Later that night, Alan Arthur, now a college student in New York, joined his father. Friends went to find a judge and returned with John R. Brady, a justice of the New York Supreme Court. Someone scribbled the presidential oath on a piece of paper. In the early morning hours of September 20, Chester A. Arthur was sworn in as the 21st president of the United States.

Chapter 5

A Good Start

As the new president, Arthur had much to overcome. He was condemned and mistrusted by many in his own party, and his Democratic opponents pictured him as a corrupt machine politician.

At the same time, many observers had been impressed by Arthur's dignified behavior during the months when Garfield was fighting for his life. The genuine grief he showed when the president died caused many to give him the benefit of the doubt. Friendly newspapers tried to show him in a favorable light. The *New York Sun* wrote, "While Mr. Arthur is not a man who would have entered anybody's mind as a direct candidate for the office, it is not at all certain that he will not make a successful administration. He is a gentleman. . . . He has tact and common sense." Another friendly report said, "The people and the politicians will find that Vice President Arthur and President Arthur are different men."

Chester Alan Arthur entered the presidency despised by many in his own party, but he surprised them by carrying out his duties honestly and effectively.

Soon after he was sworn in, Arthur proclaimed September 26, the day of Garfield's burial, a day of national mourning. Soon afterward, in a short address, Arthur pledged to be guided by Garfield's "example and experience." He asked all of Garfield's cabinet to stay on until Congress convened in December. These actions reassured the nation that he planned no sudden shifts in government policy.

The Stalwart leaders, who had been bruised by their battles with Garfield, hoped that under President Arthur they would have more opportunity to influence the government. Roscoe Conkling, now out of the Senate, let Arthur know that he would welcome appointment as secretary of state. Arthur realized that any such appointment would cause a public uproar, and promptly refused Conkling's suggestion. (He later offered to appoint Conkling to the U.S. Supreme Court, but Conkling refused the appointment.) Arthur also frustrated hopes that he would appoint a Stalwart to head the New York customhouse. Moderate William Robertson remained in that position throughout Arthur's presidency.

In December, Arthur began assembling his own cabinet. He replaced Secretary of State James G. Blaine, who had resigned, with a Stalwart Republican from New Jersey, Frederick Frelinghuysen. His other appointments to the cabinet were carefully balanced between Stalwarts and moderates. Once again, the Stalwarts were disappointed. One of them complained that Arthur "has done less for us than Garfield, or even Hayes."

Civil Service Reform

Even though Charles Guiteau was mentally ill, public accounts emphasized that he had shot President Garfield after his applications for government jobs had been refused. He was often described as a "disappointed office-seeker." Guiteau's sensational story put a spotlight on the need for reform in government appointments.

Ending the spoils system, in which jobs were awarded based on an applicant's service to a political party, was already the main goal of reform-minded Americans. In December 1880, even before Garfield and Arthur took office, Senator George Hunt Pendleton, a Democrat from Ohio, had introduced legislation in Congress calling for a new civil service board to regulate the federal government's hiring and firing of federal workers. Both parties relied on the old

Guiteau's Trial

During the early months of Arthur's term, the news was dominated by reports of Charles Guiteau's trial for the murder of President Garfield. It became painfully clear that Guiteau was mentally ill. He quizzed jurors on biblical doctrines, shouted at witnesses, and suggested that he spoke for God. He claimed that he was on close terms with Garfield, Arthur, and other high-ranking Republicans. His defense argued that he should be declared not guilty by reason of insanity, but the jury rejected the claim and sentenced him to death. Charles Guiteau died by hanging on June 30, 1882.

★ ★ ☆

system of political appointments, however, and Pendleton's proposed legislation was ignored.

By December 1881, the climate had changed. President Arthur, known to be a great "spoilsman" himself, announced his support for civil service reform in his first annual address to Congress. He declared that federal appointments should be made on the basis of applicants' abilities, and that complaints against political hiring should be investigated promptly.

During 1882, the calls for reform became louder than ever. By this point, both Republicans and Democrats were eager to gain the credit for passing some sort of reform bill. In his 1882 address to Congress, Arthur noted, "the people of the country . . . have in various ways and upon frequent occasions given expression to their earnest wish for prompt and definite action."

In 1882 a cartoon Santa Claus scolds the Congress for refusing to act on civil service reform. "Gentlemen, if you don't behave yourselves, you shall not have anything for Christmas," he says. With Arthur's support, the Pendleton Civil Service Act was passed in January 1883.

He urged the Congress to establish a civil service commission and supported ending the practice of taking "voluntary contributions" from workers. The *Chicago Tribune* reported, "In his message to Congress, President Arthur gives the order 'right about face' to the Stalwart Army."

This time, Congress responded, passing the Pendleton Civil Service Reform Act. Arthur signed the bill into law on January 16, 1883. The legislation set up a three-person commission to oversee a new merit system for awarding government jobs. Applicants would take exams, and officials who demanded "voluntary contributions" would be fined. The act did not abolish the old system overnight. In fact, it applied to only 10 percent of all government jobs, leaving many positions—including 47,000 in the post office—open for appointment by elected officials. Still, the Pendleton Act was an important first step in ending the spoils system. The civil service was broadened by later administrations to cover thousands of additional positions. Arthur's role in passing the Pendleton Act surprised many of his friends. The man who had made his fortune through the spoils system at the New York customhouse had joined the ranks of the reformers.

The Star Route Scandal

Arthur inherited another corruption scandal in the government that involved the U.S. Post Office. Postal service in settled areas of the country was provided by government employees. In the vast regions of the West, however, mail routes were awarded to private companies, which promised by contract to make mail deliveries with "certainty, celerity, and security." These private routes were marked on postal documents with stars, and so became known as the Star Routes.

The first hint of scandal arose soon after Garfield and Arthur were elected in 1881. It appeared that the process of bidding for the Star Routes was rigged. Some bids were surprisingly high, and there were suspicions that some of the money was returned, or "kicked back" to post office officials. Worse, an investigation revealed that the post office paid private companies for postal routes that didn't even exist. The trail of clues led to two prominent Stalwarts, Stephen Dorsey and Thomas Brady. When Arthur assumed office, he was faced with the unpleasant task of investigating his own political supporters. To his credit, he insisted that the investigation continue, promising to prosecute the offenders "with the utmost vigor of the law."

On March 4, 1882, a grand jury indicted nine men, including Dorsey and Brady. Unfortunately, the government's case was complicated, and the defendants engaged skilled defense lawyers to contest the charges. In September, the jury found only two defendants guilty, and Dorsey and Brady went free. In a second trial during 1883, all nine defendants were acquitted. Arthur was deeply

Postmaster General Thomas Brady, who profited from selling "star" postal routes to private contractors, is shown shaking gold stars out of a mailbag—along with a dangerous-looking scorpion that may end up biting him.

disappointed. Republicans pointed to Arthur's support for the prosecution, but Democrats pointed out that his political friends had escaped punishment. In the 1882 congressional elections, Democrats appeared to have the better argument. They won many seats in the House of Representatives, gaining a 197 to 118 majority. The Senate remained under Republican control with only a two-member majority.

Pork Barrel Politics

Today, the federal government often pays out more money in a year than it collects in taxes, causing large budget deficits. In the years following the Civil War, the situation was reversed. Every year since 1866, the federal treasury took in more money than it spent. By Arthur's presidency, the situation had become embarrassing. On June 30, 1882, the government had a surplus of $145 million.

Businessmen argued that the surplus was becoming a danger to the economy, tying up cash that could help keep the economy healthy. Many in Congress agreed, and in 1882 they put together a major bill providing $19 million for the improvement of rivers and harbors around the country. Arthur agreed in principle that government money could be used for local improvements, but he found the Rivers and Harbors Bill filled with "pork," wasteful projects designed to increase the power (and perhaps the bankrolls) of individual congressmen. On August 1, 1882, he *vetoed* the bill, sending a message to Congress listing his objections.

The Rivers and Harbors Bill had been designed to gain broad support from Congress, however. The very next day, both houses of Congress met to vote again. The bill passed by two-thirds majorities in both houses, overriding Arthur's veto, and the "pork barrel" bill became law.

The Tariff

The tariff, the tax on foreign goods imported for sale, was a critical issue through most of the 1800s. Arthur, who had been in charge of collecting tariffs in the Port of New York, was perhaps more informed about the subject than any previous president. Republicans usually favored high tariff rates. They argued that the tariffs made foreign goods more expensive and so protected U.S. manufacturers from low-price foreign competition. Democrats usually favored lower tariffs. They argued that low tariffs encouraged world trade and kept down the prices that Americans had to pay.

Arthur's Republican friends continued to favor high tariffs. Yet with a huge surplus, the federal government did not need additional income, and Arthur believed tariffs should be reduced. With support from the Senate, he created a commission to recommend tariff reductions. The commission's report recommended

The States During the Presidency of Chester A. Arthur

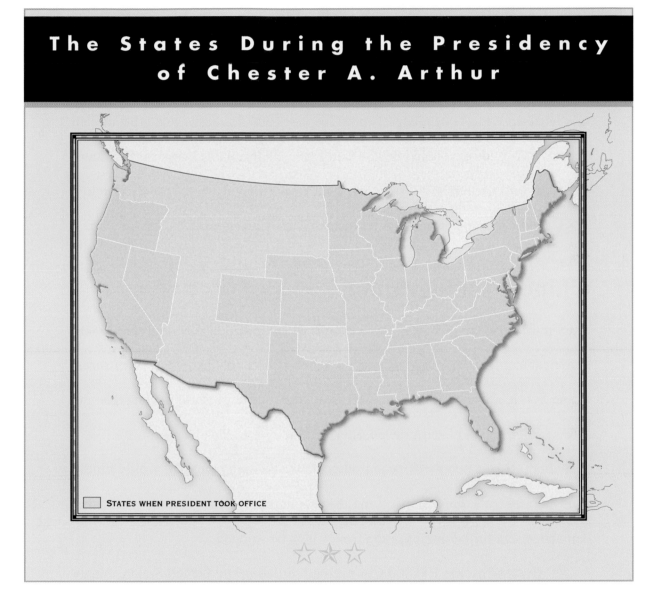

STATES WHEN PRESIDENT TOOK OFFICE

many reductions, but when the proposals were debated in Congress, one tariff rate after another was increased, under pressure from representatives who feared that a particular reduction might hurt their home district. By the end of the process, the new tariff act was a hodgepodge of tariff increases and decreases, and it pleased no one. Overall, it lowered tariffs by less than 2 percent. It became known as "the mongrel tariff bill." Arthur was disappointed with it but signed it into law on March 3, 1883. He realized that he could not expect to receive a better bill.

Chinese Immigration

Although the United States was a nation of immigrants, in the 1880s many Americans remained deeply prejudiced, especially against people of other races. In the South, African Americans were struggling unsuccessfully to preserve the civil rights they had been granted after the Civil War. Meanwhile, in the West, prejudice against people of Asian descent was growing rapidly. Anti-Chinese riots had caused serious damage and distress in San Francisco, and voters there demanded that further immigration from China be stopped.

By 1882, some 100,000 Chinese had settled in the United States, mostly in California. Many had come to work on the building of the transcontinental railroad (completed in 1869). Now many of them lived in cities, where they took up trades such as shoemaking and the manufacture of cigars. During an economic

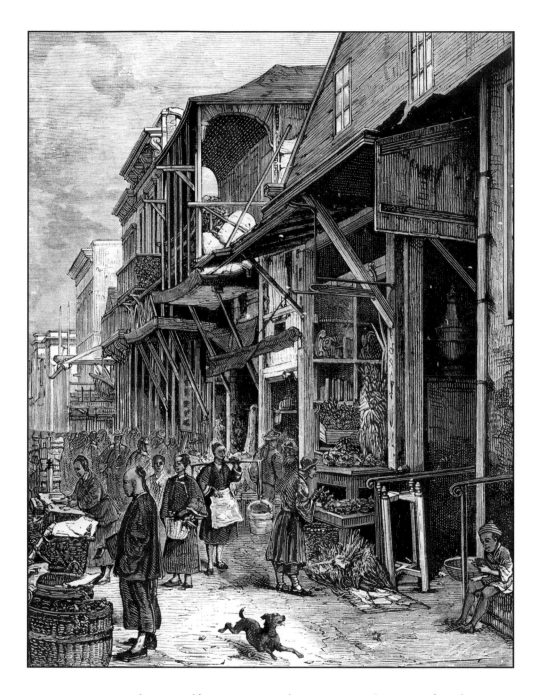

A street in San Francisco's Chinatown. Californians were urging the government to end immigration from China.

downturn in the 1870s, westerners began to favor laws that would bar more Chinese from entering the country. In 1880, President Hayes negotiated a treaty with China that allowed the United States to limit Chinese immigration.

Responding to demands for further limitations, Congress passed a bill in 1882 to exclude all immigration from China for 20 years and to deny U.S. citizenship to immigrants born in China. Arthur did not oppose some further restriction on Chinese immigration, but he believed that the bill violated the treaty of 1880. He also thought that 20 years was too long a period. He vetoed the bill, causing a

Native Americans

By the time Arthur became president, most Native Americans were confined to reservations in remote territories. They still presented a serious problem for the U.S. government, however. Reports of their poverty and neglect by corrupt government agents sparked a debate on Native American policy. Like many at the time, Arthur believed that Indians deserved to be United States citizens, but he thought that they would not achieve citizenship until they adopted modern ways. "Their hunting days are over," he said. To help Native Americans enter mainstream society, Arthur earmarked extra money for education and training in farming and manufacturing. He encouraged individual Native Americans to leave their reservations and offered land grants to those who left to take up farming or trade. More than 11,000 grants were made during his presidency.

☆ ☆ ☆

furious reaction from labor groups in the West, who were seeking to preserve jobs for non-Asian workers. Congress soon revised the bill so that it excluded Chinese immigration for ten years. The bill still contained provisions that Arthur found objectionable, but he signed it into law. At the same time, Arthur's secretary of state, Frederick Frelinghuysen, assured China's representative in Washington that he would do all he could to curb future anti-Chinese violence.

The Navy

During the late 1800s, major European nations began assembling worldwide empires, claiming colonies in Asia and Africa. To establish and defend these colonies, they relied increasingly on powerful navies. It was clear to American traders and businessmen that European countries were gaining control of world trade and that the United States was not keeping up.

After the Civil War, the U.S. Navy had been neglected. By 1881, it had become a disaster, described by one historian as "a *flotilla* of death-traps and defenseless antiques." The United States did not possess a single modern warship. Of its fleet of 200, not one had a high-powered cannon and most were made of wood instead of steel. Many naval commanders treated their ships as their own private yachts, and the Navy Department was staffed by people who knew nothing about ships.

The USS *Boston*, one of the first modern metal-clad steam-driven warships in the U.S. Navy, was authorized by the Arthur administration. In this photograph, the crew is standing in the rigging during a naval parade.

In 1881, James Garfield's secretary of the navy, Judge William H. Hunt, set up a planning board to survey the navy's needs, and it recommended that 68 new steel ships be constructed. Arthur's navy secretary, William E. Chandler, closed obsolete navy yards, made plans for new navy gun foundries, and organized the Naval War College at Newport, Rhode Island. In an address to Congress in 1884, Arthur warned: "The long peace that has lulled us into a sense of fancied security may at any time be disturbed." He urged that the United States begin strengthening its navy. Congress appropriated money for two new cruisers and two new gunboats. It also passed an act prohibiting the repair of outdated navy ships. As a result, many navy ships were junked. Secretary Chandler said, "I think that I did my best work in destroying the old navy."

Construction began on the ships authorized by Congress, but they were not launched until after Arthur left office. Named *Atlanta*, *Boston*, *Chicago*, and *Dolphin*, they were popularly known as the "ABCD" ships. Giving the navy its first major push toward modernization was one of Arthur's most important accomplishments.

Chapter 6

A Well-Liked Leader

Life in the White House ——————

Before moving into the Executive Mansion, Arthur undertook a major spring cleaning. He had 24 wagonloads of furniture and odds and ends carted off to be sold at public auction. Among the objects were a pair of Abraham Lincoln's trousers and a birdcage that belonged to Nellie Grant, President Grant's daughter. Arthur then engaged fashionable New York designer Louis Comfort Tiffany to redecorate the house. Tiffany's designs included paneling made of Japanese leather and art objects from China. Arthur also installed indoor plumbing and elevators.

Presidents Hayes and Garfield had entertained sparingly. By contrast, Chester Arthur enjoyed lavish social occasions. He often invited guests to dinner and served as host at many larger parties and receptions. During the busiest part of the social season, Arthur's

Arthur contributed to beautifying and redesigning parts of the White House. The north entrance features stained glass designed by the famous designer Louis Comfort Tiffany.

youngest sister, Mary McElroy, came from Albany to serve as White House hostess. The formal dinners were prepared by a French chef and could include up to 14 courses. Sometimes the gatherings got out of control. Toward the end of his term, one reception became so crowded that an important general was forced to enter the White House through a window. On another occasion, Arthur had to make his way through a crowd of 3,000 to reach the Blue Room.

Arthur's sister, Mrs. Mary McElroy, served as White House hostess during his term of office.

For relaxation, Arthur enjoyed riding around Washington in his elegant horse-drawn carriage. Built in New York, it was dark green, with cloth trimmings. The dress blankets and lap robes bore the monogram *CAA*. The horses were handsome, and the coach-man was always well dressed. As he rode around town, Arthur acknowledged all passersby, regardless of their social position, by tipping his hat and bowing. Wherever he went, Arthur was admired for his fine taste in clothing. He wore tweeds during business hours, frock coats in the afternoon, and a tuxedo at dinner. One admirer said, "It is his ease, polish, and perfect manner that make him the greatest society lion we have had in many years."

Arthur was a sociable president partly because he had little family life at the White House. After his wife's death in 1880, the Arthur children lived with relatives in New York. Although they visited the White House, they did not live there for long periods. Meanwhile, the public showed a great interest in the president's private life. When it was reported that fresh flowers were placed in front of a woman's portrait each day in the White House, people speculated that the president was having a romance. Newspapers later reported that the portrait was of Arthur's late wife, Nell. Arthur resented curiosity about his personal activities. Once when a woman asked if he was seeing a woman, he snapped, "Madam, I may be president of the United States, but my private life is nobody's damned business!"

Presidential Business

As president, Arthur kept a relaxed schedule. He arrived in his office around 10 o'clock in the morning and received many visitors during the day. He met with his cabinet twice a week and greeted the public three times a week for an hour. Though Arthur established a solid record as president, his staff complained that

As James Garfield lay dying, Arthur received a letter from a woman in New York City named Julia Sand. It began: "The hours of Garfield's life are numbered—before this meets your eye, you may be President. The people are bowed in grief; but—do you realize it?—not so much because he is dying, as because *you* are his successor. . . . Great emergencies awaken generous traits which have lain dormant half a life."

Arthur received many more equally blunt letters from Julia, urging him to be a good president and to pursue a course of reform. Intrigued, Arthur wrote back often. Finally, in November 20, 1882, he paid Julia a surprise visit at her home. The president and his mystery correspondent talked for a full hour. Julia Sand was the daughter of a New York banker. She and Arthur had never met until he visited her in 1882. As far as we know, they never met again.

☆☆☆

he was not always quick to make decisions. One White House clerk said, "President Arthur never did today what he could put off until tomorrow."

The President's Health

Even before he had served as president for a year, President Arthur began to feel ill. Sometime during 1882, his doctors told him that he had Bright's disease, a kidney ailment that was almost always fatal. In January 1883, a reporter noted that Arthur had "grown thin and feeble looking." That same year he wrote to his son, "I have been so ill since the adjournment [of Congress] that I have hardly been able to dispose of the accumulation of business still before me." Still, Arthur was determined not to make his illness public.

In 1883, Arthur traveled widely despite his declining health. In May 1883, he attended the ceremonies opening the Brooklyn Bridge. Then the longest suspension bridge in the world, it crossed the East River from New York City to Brooklyn. As a longtime New Yorker, Arthur was proud of the monumental bridge and was a center of attention during the celebrations.

That summer Arthur traveled west to visit Yellowstone National Park, hoping that a vacation there might improve his health. With a party of friends, he undertook a three-week trek through the park on horseback, taking time to enjoy fishing in the mountain streams. One day Arthur and a friend caught 105 pounds (48 kilograms) of fish!

The trip seemed to do the president some good. On his way home, he stopped in Chicago and was greeted by a huge crowd. He shook hands with well-wishers for several hours, which left him completely exhausted. It was clear to his traveling companions that he had not recovered from his illness. Yet none of his political supporters except Secretary of State Frelinghuysen knew how serious his medical condition was.

Arthur returned to New York in May 1883 to help dedicate the Brooklyn Bridge, then the world's longest suspension bridge, which connected New York City to Brooklyn.

Election of 1884

Most presidents during peaceful times are favorites to be nominated to run again. Arthur was an exception. Even though his harshest critics admitted that Arthur had done a better job as president than expected, he had little support for renomination. The moderates still did not trust him and favored nominating their leader, James G. Blaine. The Stalwarts were still angry that Arthur had refused to appoint his old allies to high positions. In addition, a growing number of young reformers in the party did not trust Arthur even though he had signed the Pendleton Act and pressed for prosecutions in the Star Route scandal.

Arthur himself had mixed feelings about the nomination. He knew that it was unlikely he would live through a second term. Even so, he resented his party's rejection, and he did not want to cast doubt on his ability to continue in his duties. He decided to stay in the race, but he told loyal supporters that he was not really eager to receive the nomination. At the Republican convention in June 1884, the moderates took control and nominated James Blaine easily. Although Arthur had never liked Blaine, he pledged his "earnest and cordial support." That fall, Blaine was deserted by reform Republicans and lost an extremely close election to Democrat Grover Cleveland.

In the final days of his administration, on February 22, 1885, Arthur presided over the dedication of the Washington Monument a few blocks from the

On February 22, 1885, Arthur helped dedicate the Washington Monument, which had been under construction for nearly 37 years.

White House. The huge obelisk, standing more than 555 feet (169 m) high, was dedicated on the 153rd birthday of the nation's first president.

Arthur's last official act was to sign a bill granting former president Ulysses S. Grant the full benefits of a retired general. Grant, who was dying of cancer, had suffered serious financial disasters and was nearly broke. The pension was intended to provide support for his family after his death. Congress passed the bill only a few moments before the congressional session ended. The Capitol clock was set back six minutes to give Arthur time to sign it into law. When he had signed, the members of the Senate and House of Representatives burst into cheers.

Legacy

Upon leaving the White House, Arthur was asked about his plans. Not taking the question seriously, he replied with a smile, "Well, there doesn't seem anything else for an ex-president to do but to go into the country and raise big pumpkins."

Arthur retired to his home in New York City. He hoped to return to practicing law, but he was not well enough. Less than two years after leaving the White House, he died on November 18, 1886, surrounded by his sisters and children. The *New York Times* wrote, "No duty was neglected by his administration, and no adventurous project alarmed the nation. There was no scandal to make us

Statue in Madison Square Park

In 1899, a statue of Arthur was unveiled in New York City's Madison Square Park, not far from his home. At the dedication, Elihu Root said, "He was wise in statesmanship and firm and effective in administration." Observant visitors today may notice that Arthur's statue seems to look across the park toward a statue of Roscoe Conkling, his longtime mentor and sometime enemy. Conkling died less than three years after Arthur.

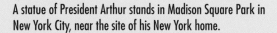
A statue of President Arthur stands in Madison Square Park in New York City, near the site of his New York home.

☆ ★ ☆

ashamed while he was in office and none to be ripped up when he went out of it. He earned and deserved the honest fame he possesses."

Chester Arthur remains one of America's great political surprises. On the day President Garfield died, most Americans expected Arthur, a man entrenched in New York machine politics, to appoint his friends to high offices and to oppose government reforms. Instead, Arthur governed fairly and openly supported reform, especially in the way that government jobs were awarded. Newspaper publisher Alexander McClure wrote, "No man ever entered the presidency so profoundly and widely distrusted as Chester Alan Arthur, and no one ever retired from the highest civil trust of the world more generally respected, alike by political friend and foe."

Arthur might be better known today—for all the wrong reasons—if he had behaved as people expected. Instead, Arthur's steady but unspectacular administration is often overlooked. He deserves at least the credit for holding the best interests of the country above his allegiance to old political friends.

Chester Arthur's burial place in the Albany Rural Cemetery just north of the New York State capital.

Fast Facts
Chester A. Arthur

Birth:	October 5, 1829
Birthplace:	Fairfield, Vermont
Parents:	William Arthur and Malvina Stone Arthur
Brothers & Sisters:	Regina (1822–?)
	Jane (1824–?)
	Almeda (?–?)
	Ann Eliza (?–?)
	Malvina (?–?)
	William (1834–1915)
	George (1836–?)
	Mary (?–1916)
Education:	Union College; graduated 1848
Occupations:	Lawyer, administrator
Marriage:	To Ellen "Nell" Lewis Herndon, October 25, 1859
Children:	(see First Lady Fast Facts at right)
Political Party:	Republican
Public Offices:	1862–1863 Quartermaster General of the State of New York
	1871–1878 Collector of the Port of New York
	1881 Vice President of the United States
	1881–1885 21st President of the United States
His Vice President:	None
Major Actions as President:	1882 Signed the Chinese Exclusion Act
	1883 Signed the Pendleton Act, first law reforming U.S. civil service
	1883 Signed act to modernize U.S. Navy
Firsts:	First native of Vermont to serve as president
Death:	November 18, 1886
Age at Death:	57
Burial Place:	Albany Rural Cemetery, Menands, New York

Fast Facts Ellen (Nell) Herndon

Birth:	August 30, 1837
Birthplace:	Culpeper Court House, Virginia
Parents:	William L. Herndon and Frances Hansbrough Herndon
Brothers & Sisters:	None
Education:	Unknown
Marriage:	To Chester Alan Arthur, October 25, 1859
Children:	William Lewis Herndon (1860–1863)
	Chester Alan Jr. (Alan) (1864–1937)
	Ellen Herndon (Nell) (1871–1915)
Death:	January 12, 1880 (before Arthur became president)
Age at Death:	42
Burial Place:	Albany Rural Cemetery, Menands, New York

Timeline

1829	1845	1848	1853	1854
Chester A. Arthur born October 5 in Fairfield, Vermont	Enters Union College, Schenectady, New York	Graduates from Union College; becomes a schoolteacher in New York and Vermont	Moves to New York City to study law	Licensed to practice law

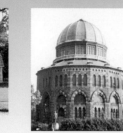

1861	1862	1863	1864	1869
Civil War begins	Arthur is appointed quartermaster general of New York, in charge of providing for state troops	Son William dies	Son Chester Alan Jr. born	Arthur is appointed counsel to the New York City Tax Commission

1881	1881	1882	1883	1884
President Garfield shot, July; Garfield dies September 19, Arthur sworn in as president September 20	Arthur announces support for civil service reform, December	Signs Chinese Exclusion Act	Signs the Pendleton Act, reforming federal civil service; signs bill to modernize U.S. Navy	James G. Blaine receives Republican presidential nomination, June; Democrat Grover Cleveland elected, November

1855	1856	1857	1859	1860
Successfully represents Elizabeth Jennings in racial discrimination suit	Campaigns for John C. Frémont, first Republican nominee for president	Engaged to Ellen (Nell) Herndon; visits Kansas Territory	Marries Nell Herndon, October 25	Son William born

1871	1878	1880	1880	1881
Appointed Collector of the Port of New York, in charge of the New York customhouse; daughter Ellen (Nell) born	Arthur suspended as Collector of the Port by President Hayes, after charges of corruption	Wife Nell dies, January	Arthur receives Republican nomination for vice president, June; elected with President James Garfield, November	Arthur and Garfield take office, March

1885	1886
Arthur dedicates Washington Monument, February; leaves office, March	Arthur dies of kidney disease in New York City

Glossary

abolitionist: in the mid-1800s, a person who believed that slavery should be outlawed in the United States

attorney general: the highest ranking law enforcement officer in the U.S. federal government

balanced ticket: nominees (as for president and vice president) chosen to appeal to voters from different party factions or different regions of the country

ceremonial position: a job or office that is mostly for show and involves little responsibility or authority

emancipate: to grant freedom under the law to slaves

flotilla: a fleet, or group, of ships

merit: worth or ability; civil service reformers believed that government jobs should be awarded on the basis of merit, including education and experience, rather than on party membership

secede: (of a state or other political unit) to withdraw from a larger political unit; the southern states seceded from the United States

spoils system: in U.S. politics, the practice of awarding government jobs and contracts only to party members to reward their services and loyalty

tariff: a tax on goods imported into the country for sale

veto: the refusal of a president to refuse to sign a bill passed by Congress into law; Congress may override a veto by passing it by two-thirds majorities in both the House and the Senate

vigilante: a person who takes the law into his or her own hands, often by imposing punishment on a person who has been accused but not convicted of a crime

Further Reading

Joseph, Paul. *Chester Arthur*. Edina, MN: Checkerboard Library, 2000.

Santella, Andrew. *Chester A. Arthur*. Minneapolis, MN: Compass Point Books, 2003.

Stevens, Rita. *Chester A. Arthur, 21st President of the United States*. Ada, OK: Garrett Educational Publishing, 1989.

Young, Jeff C. *Chester A. Arthur*. Berkeley Heights, NJ: Enslow Publications, 2002

MORE ADVANCED READING

Cunliffe, Marcus. *The Presidency*. 3rd edition. Boston: Houghton Mifflin, 1987.

Doenecke, Justus D. *The Presidencies of James A. Garfield and Chester A. Arthur*. Lawrence: University Press of Kansas, 1981.

Gould, Lewis. *Grand Old Party: A History of the Republicans*. New York: Random House, 2003.

Howe, George Frederick. *Chester A. Arthur: A Quarter-Century of Machine Politics*. New York: F. Unger, 1935.

Karabell, Zachary. *Chester A. Arthur*. New York: Times Books, 2004.

Reeves, Thomas C. *Gentleman Boss: The Life of Chester Alan Arthur*. New York: Alfred A. Knopf, 1975.

Places to Visit

President Chester A. Arthur State Historical Site
Fairfield, VT
(802) 828-3051

A re-creation of the house in which Arthur is believed to have been born in this small community north of Burlington, Vermont. Nearby is a small Baptist church on the site of the church where Arthur's father served.

Madison Square Park
Bounded by Fifth Avenue, Madison Avenue, 23rd Street, and 26th Street
New York, NY

Life-size statues of Chester A. Arthur and his mentor Roscoe Conkling stand opposite each other in the park.

The White House
1600 Pennsylvania Avenue NW
Washington, DC 20500
(202) 456-7041

Arthur lived here from late 1881 to March 1885 and took a strong hand in renovating the mansion.

Online Sites of Interest

★ **Arthur Birthplace**

www.dhca.state.vt.us/HistoricSites/html/arthur.html

Provides brief information on Arthur's birthplace.

★ **The White House**

http://www.whitehouse.gov/history/presidents/ca21.html

Provides a brief biography of President Arthur. The White House site also offers lots of additional information on White House history, first ladies, and the presidency today.

★ **Presidents of the United States (IPL POTUS)**

http://www.ipl.org/div/potus/caarthur.html

Provides essential information on Arthur and links to other sites of interest. Site is managed by the University of Michigan School of Information.

★ **American Presidency (Grolier)**

http://ap.grolier.com/

Biographies of all the presidents at different reading levels from this publisher of encyclopedias and other reference works.

★ **American President**

http://www.americanpresident.org/history/chesterccrthur/

Provides an extended biography of President Arthur and additional information on his cabinet members and administration. The site is managed by the Miller Center of Public Affairs at the University of Virginia.

★ **History of the causes leading up to the Pendleton Act**

www.classbrain.com/artteenst/publish/article_130.shtml

A useful introduction to the issue of civil service reform in the late 1800s.

Table of Presidents

	1. George Washington	2. John Adams	3. Thomas Jefferson	4. James Madison
Took office	Apr 30 1789	Mar 4 1797	Mar 4 1801	Mar 4 1809
Left office	Mar 3 1797	Mar 3 1801	Mar 3 1809	Mar 3 1817
Birthplace	Westmoreland Co, VA	Braintree, MA	Shadwell, VA	Port Conway, VA
Birth date	Feb 22 1732	Oct 20 1735	Apr 13 1743	Mar 16 1751
Death date	Dec 14 1799	July 4 1826	July 4 1826	June 28 1836

	9. William H. Harrison	10. John Tyler	11. James K. Polk	12. Zachary Taylor
Took office	Mar 4 1841	Apr 6 1841	Mar 4 1845	Mar 5 1849
Left office	**Apr 4 1841•**	Mar 3 1845	Mar 3 1849	**July 9 1850•**
Birthplace	Berkeley, VA	Greenway, VA	Mecklenburg Co, NC	Barboursville, VA
Birth date	Feb 9 1773	Mar 29 1790	Nov 2 1795	Nov 24 1784
Death date	Apr 4 1841	Jan 18 1862	June 15 1849	July 9 1850

	17. Andrew Johnson	18. Ulysses S. Grant	19. Rutherford B. Hayes	20. James A. Garfield
Took office	Apr 15 1865	Mar 4 1869	Mar 5 1877	Mar 4 1881
Left office	Mar 3 1869	Mar 3 1877	Mar 3 1881	**Sept 19 1881•**
Birthplace	Raleigh, NC	Point Pleasant, OH	Delaware, OH	Orange, OH
Birth date	Dec 29 1808	Apr 27 1822	Oct 4 1822	Nov 19 1831
Death date	July 31 1875	July 23 1885	Jan 17 1893	Sept 19 1881

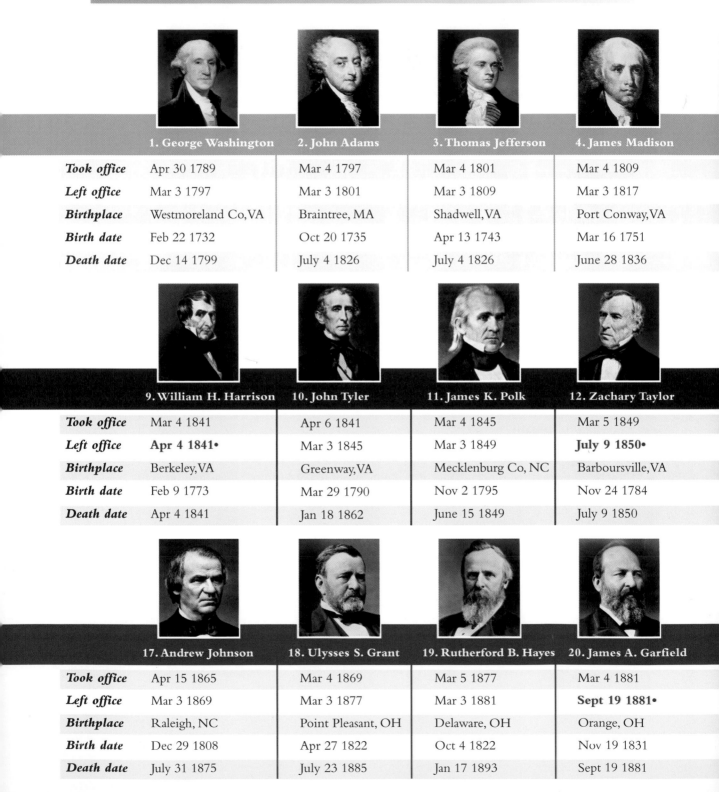

5. James Monroe	6. John Quincy Adams	7. Andrew Jackson	8. Martin Van Buren
Mar 4 1817	Mar 4 1825	Mar 4 1829	Mar 4 1837
Mar 3 1825	Mar 3 1829	Mar 3 1837	Mar 3 1841
Westmoreland Co, VA	Braintree, MA	The Waxhaws, SC	Kinderhook, NY
Apr 28 1758	July 11 1767	Mar 15 1767	Dec 5 1782
July 4 1831	Feb 23 1848	June 8 1845	July 24 1862

13. Millard Fillmore	14. Franklin Pierce	15. James Buchanan	16. Abraham Lincoln
July 9 1850	Mar 4 1853	Mar 4 1857	Mar 4 1861
Mar 3 1853	Mar 3 1857	Mar 3 1861	**Apr 15 1865•**
Locke Township, NY	Hillsborough, NH	Cove Gap, PA	Hardin Co, KY
Jan 7 1800	Nov 23 1804	Apr 23 1791	Feb 12 1809
Mar 8 1874	Oct 8 1869	June 1 1868	Apr 15 1865

21. Chester A. Arthur	22. Grover Cleveland	23. Benjamin Harrison	24. Grover Cleveland
Sept 19 1881	Mar 4 1885	Mar 4 1889	Mar 4 1893
Mar 3 1885	Mar 3 1889	Mar 3 1893	Mar 3 1897
Fairfield, VT	Caldwell, NJ	North Bend, OH	Caldwell, NJ
Oct 5 1829	Mar 18 1837	Aug 20 1833	Mar 18 1837
Nov 18 1886	June 24 1908	Mar 13 1901	June 24 1908

	25. William McKinley	**26. Theodore Roosevelt**	**27. William H. Taft**	**28. Woodrow Wilson**
Took office	Mar 4 1897	Sept 14 1901	Mar 4 1909	Mar 4 1913
Left office	**Sept 14 1901•**	Mar 3 1909	Mar 3 1913	Mar 3 1921
Birthplace	Niles, OH	New York, NY	Cincinnati, OH	Staunton, VA
Birth date	Jan 29 1843	Oct 27 1858	Sept 15 1857	Dec 28 1856
Death date	Sept 14 1901	Jan 6 1919	Mar 8 1930	Feb 3 1924

	33. Harry S. Truman	**34. Dwight D. Eisenhower**	**35. John F. Kennedy**	**36. Lyndon B. Johnson**
Took office	Apr 12 1945	Jan 20 1953	Jan 20 1961	Nov 22 1963
Left office	Jan 20 1953	Jan 20 1961	**Nov 22 1963•**	Jan 20 1969
Birthplace	Lamar, MO	Denison, TX	Brookline, MA	Johnson City, TX
Birth date	May 8 1884	Oct 14 1890	May 29 1917	Aug 27 1908
Death date	Dec 26 1972	Mar 28 1969	Nov 22 1963	Jan 22 1973

	41. George Bush	**42. Bill Clinton**	**43. George W. Bush**	
Took office	Jan 20 1989	Jan 20 1993	Jan 20 2001	
Left office	Jan 20 1993	Jan 20 2001	—	
Birthplace	Milton, MA	Hope, AR	New Haven, CT	
Birth date	June 12 1924	Aug 19 1946	July 6 1946	
Death date	—	—	—	

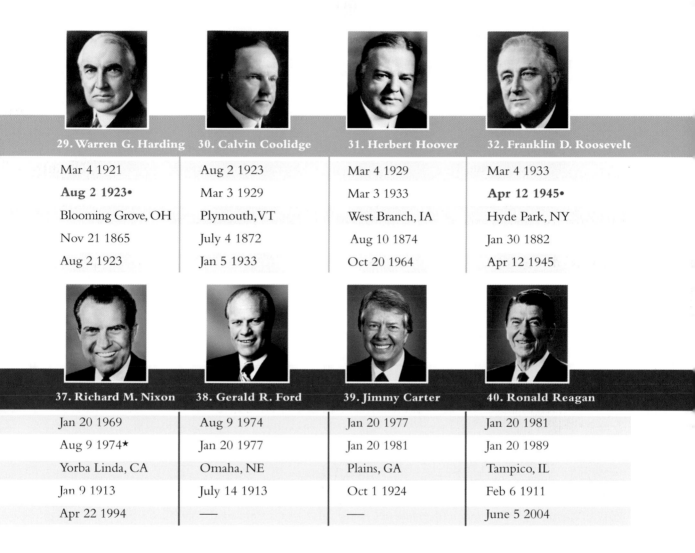

29. Warren G. Harding	30. Calvin Coolidge	31. Herbert Hoover	32. Franklin D. Roosevelt
Mar 4 1921	Aug 2 1923	Mar 4 1929	Mar 4 1933
Aug 2 1923•	Mar 3 1929	Mar 3 1933	**Apr 12 1945•**
Blooming Grove, OH	Plymouth, VT	West Branch, IA	Hyde Park, NY
Nov 21 1865	July 4 1872	Aug 10 1874	Jan 30 1882
Aug 2 1923	Jan 5 1933	Oct 20 1964	Apr 12 1945

37. Richard M. Nixon	38. Gerald R. Ford	39. Jimmy Carter	40. Ronald Reagan
Jan 20 1969	Aug 9 1974	Jan 20 1977	Jan 20 1981
Aug 9 1974★	Jan 20 1977	Jan 20 1981	Jan 20 1989
Yorba Linda, CA	Omaha, NE	Plains, GA	Tampico, IL
Jan 9 1913	July 14 1913	Oct 1 1924	Feb 6 1911
Apr 22 1994	—	—	June 5 2004

• Indicates the president died while in office.

★ Richard Nixon resigned before his term expired.

Index

★ ★ ★ ★ ★

New York customhouse, 38, 39, *41,* 44, 45, 67
New York State
    Garfield election, 55
    legislature, 59
    militia, 25, 26, 28, 30–31
    political parties, 34
    Republican party, 23–24, 35, 37, 43

Paine, Judge Elijah, 16
party organizations. *See* machine politics
Pendleton Civil Service Reform Act, 8, 68, 70
percentage system, 40
Platt, Thomas, 59
pork barrel politics, 73–74
Port of New York, 39, 58
Post Office, United States, 70, 71
Powell, Alec, 63
press
    attacks on Arthur, 39, 53, 58, 61
    support for Arthur, 55, 65, 70, 92, 94

quartermaster general, office of (New York
        State), 26–31

reform, political
    civil service, 68, 69, *69*
    Hayes, Rutherford B., 44
    Republican party, 38, 90
Republican party. *See also* moderates,
        Republican; Stalwarts
    customhouse appointments, 38, 39–40
    formation, 23
    New York City, 23, 37
    New York State, 23–24, 34, 35, 37, 43, 46
    nomination of Garfield, 52
    presidential race of 1880, 50–56
    reformers, 38, 90

Rivers and Harbors Bill (1882), 73–74
Robertson, William H., 58, 59, 67

San Francisco, California, Chinese in, 76, *77*
Sand, Julia, 87
scandal. *See* corruption, political
slavery, 10, 11, 14, 16, 21, 23
spoils system, 24, 37, 43
Stalwarts, 49, 50, 61, 90
    during Arthur administration, 67
    Garfield administration, 56, 57, 58
    Star Route Scandal, 71
    Treaty of Fifth Avenue, 55
Star Route Scandal, 70–71
states during Arthur presidency, map of, 75
Stillman, Asa, 12
Stone, Malvina, 10

tariffs, 39, 74, 76
Tax Commission, New York City, 37
Tiffany, Louis Comfort, 83
Tilden, Samuel, 43, 44
Treaty of Fifth Avenue, 55
Twain, Mark, 8
Tweed, William "Boss," 38, 43

Union College (New York), 12, *13,* 14

vice president, responsibilities of, 53, 55

Washington Monument, 90, *91,* 92
Weed, Thurlow, 23–24, *24,* 25
Whig party, 22–23
White House, 83, *84,* 85
Wilson, Billy, 28–29

Yellowstone National Park, 88

About the Author

Dan Elish is the author of numerous novels and nonfiction books for young readers, including *Born Too Short: Confessions of an 8th Grade Basket Case*, which was chosen among Books for the Teen Age 2003 by the New York Public Library. Dan has also written scripts for the TV show *Cyberchase* and the music and lyrics for several musicals. He lives in New York City with his wife and daughter.